LESSONS FROM THE
JAPANESE MASTERS

Fred Neff

**Photographs by James Reid
and Patrick O'Leary**

Lerner Publications Company • Minneapolis

To my wonderful friend and wife, Christa Neff, whose love, help,
and support is greatly appreciated.

The models photographed in this book are Christa Neff, Richard DeValerio, Jim
Reid, William McLeod, Elias Murdock, Helena Koudelka, and Peter Koudelka.

Japanese calligraphy on back cover by Kenichi Tazawa.

Library of Congress Cataloging-in-Publication Data
Neff, Fred.
    Lessons from the Japanese masters / by Fred Neff.
        p. cm.
    Includes index.
    Summary: Examines the history and philosophy of Japanese martial
arts and gives instruction in a variety of related self-defense
techniques.
    ISBN 0-8225-1164-9 (lib. bdg.)
    1. Self-defense for children—Juvenile literature. 2. Martial
arts—Juvenile literature. [1. Self-defense. 2. Martial arts.]
I. Reid, James, ill. II. O'Leary, Patrick, ill. III. Title.
GV1111.4.N44 1995
796.8—dc20   92-8922
                                                                CIP
                                                                 AC

Manufactured in the United States of America
1 2 3 4 5 6 – I/SF – 00 99 98 97 96 95

CONTENTS

1

INTRODUCTION

Why do businesspeople and martial-arts enthusiasts both study the teachings of the ancient Japanese masters of self-defense? One important reason is that the Japanese masters knew far more than just how to handle a street fight. The lessons taught by these learned people can improve not only your self-defense abilities but also many aspects of your life—your health, your interactions with other people, your business practices, and much more.

The ancient masters taught how to cope with the greatest opponent we face—ourselves. Once you learn to manage your inner feelings, you can free energy for handling other problems, including a physical attack by an aggressor. Success in fighting depends on conserving energy for protection. That kind of self-control is useful in many situations, in addition to combat. Although you should first look at each of the lessons in this book as a self-defense approach, you should later try to see how the attitude and control you have learned can be used for other purposes as well.

Actor Matsumoto Koshiro as Samurai. Color woodblock print. Katsukawa Shunko, Japanese, 1743–1812.

©The Cleveland Museum of Art, The Kelvin Smith Collection, Gift of Mrs. Kelvin Smith, 85.350

Some teachers of one martial art, *kempo*, tell this legend to beginning students. In ancient times, a young warrior who had been very successful in battle was traveling along a road. He encountered a peasant who was blocking his path, and attempted to push the man aside. The warrior immediately found himself on the ground. No matter what he did, he was helpless against the defenses of the peasant.

Finally, in exasperation he asked how a common peasant could perform such feats. "My ability," the peasant replied, "comes from what I have been taught by the old master in the village." Intrigued, the warrior traveled to the modest home of the master, knocked at the door, and was invited in by a frail old man.

After sitting down to tea, the young guest bragged about his great skill and his many successes in battle. The master silently took a teacup, poured hot tea into it. He kept on pouring until the tea overflowed and spilled onto the young man's lap. "You careless old man!" the warrior exclaimed. "They call you a great master, but you can't even fill a teacup properly." The master smiled and replied, "The cup, young man, is much like your mind—so full that anything else put into it will only spill out."

At times we are all like the young warrior—so full of what we know that no new knowledge can stay with us. Approach the lessons of the Japanese masters with an open mind, allowing yourself to see the many ad-vantages that can come from understanding them. The objective of this book is not just to expose you to self-defense skills, but to explain the formula the Japanese masters left us for the development of human potential.

Obviously, no book could include all the teachings of the many Japanese masters throughout history. Instead, this book relates some of the significant lessons. Continue your study by taking lessons from a qualified martial-arts instructor.

One of the traditional ways to teach Japanese martial arts is to introduce techniques for handling a particular type of threatening situation. In this way, a student learns both a technique and its practical use in a real situation.

The situational lesson plan given later in this book also gets students to think about and practice combinations of moves to respond to a confrontation. The use of combinations is important because a single isolated move may not end a fight. In addition, no two aggressors and no two fights are exactly alike. If you cannot easily combine techniques to respond to a threat, your adversary may be able to exploit a gap in your defenses.

Study carefully and learn all of the fighting techniques introduced in this book—both individually and in combination—while keeping your mind open to adapting these moves to other possible circumstances. This book will not only help you learn to defend yourself, but it also will give you greater insight into the many benefits of martial-arts training.

CHAPTER
2

HISTORY

Japan was not always a world leader. In early times, Japan was not even a nation, but a group of islands whose people were constantly at war with themselves and with others. Although historical records are unclear about exactly when Japan was first unified, it appears that some time in the seventh century, one leader finally gained enough power to be considered emperor of the islands that we now call Japan.

Unification, however, did not mean peace. Warfare continued as different groups and families struggled for power and control of the limited land and resources of Japan. Out of this struggle, the Japanese martial arts we know today were born.

The warriors who fought in the struggles of this period often used weapons, but they also developed weaponless techniques for close hand-to-hand fighting. Weaponless fighting at this time usually involved various combinations of headbutts, holds, wrestling moves, and blows with the hands and feet. One of the earliest weaponless techniques we know of is called *kumi-uchi.* Another early school of fighting was called *sumai,* a very distant ancestor of the modern (and far more refined) sport of sumo wrestling.

By the eighth century, skilled fighters became a separate class in Japanese society known as the *bushi.* These warrior nobles were lower in status than the emperor's family but higher than ordinary people. Some bushi families grew very powerful—so powerful that their leaders, known as *daimyo,* commanded their own private armies and controlled their own domains within the empire. The soldiers who served in a daimyo's army were called *samurai,* meaning "those who serve."

Even at this early stage in Japanese history (about the 12th century) the influence of the samurai was strong. As one group of samurai or another battled its way to national dominance, its leader became *shogun.* A shogun was a warlord who was supposedly under the authority of the emperor, but who in reality was the military head of government.

By this time, Japanese fighting techniques had evolved a great deal. In the West, people tend to view fighting as a strictly physical endeavor. In the Japanese view, however, success in battle depends on mental and spiritual factors as well.

This view led to the development in Japan of such refined fighting arts as *tai-jutsu* and *yawara.* Tai-jutsu, which means "body art," is the more important of the two. Unlike many other fighting methods in early Japan, tai-jutsu was a complete martial art instead of a set of fighting techniques and tricks for battle. As early as A.D. 800, tai-jutsu included philosophy, tactics for warfare, a code of health practices, and a complete method of self-defense.

Tai-jutsu philosophy, based on the Japanese Shinto religious belief that people must be in harmony with their environment, taught that fighting techniques must be natural, effective, and consistent with the best current medical knowledge. The belief that techniques should be natural did not, however, rule out the use of weapons to complement the tai-jutsu techniques of grappling, holds, headbutting, punching, striking, and kicking. In fact, as Japanese technology evolved, warriors increasingly used bows and arrows, swords, halberds, and spears as their primary instruments of battle. Kumi-uchi, yawara, tai-jutsu, and other body-oriented fighting arts were still practiced, but mostly as backups for combat with weapons. The samurai, who contributed much to the development of unarmed fighting arts, used them mostly to supplement archery or swordwork.

Another group of martial-arts practitioners in Japan—the warrior priests—successfully blended religious belief and fighting skill. We may not now usually think of holy men as warriors, but in 12th-century Japan the con-

A painting of Japanese masters

nection was not unusual. The warrior priests followed Buddhism, a religion that had earlier spread from the Chinese mainland to Japan. These Japanese priests blended a type of Buddhism (known in China as Chan and in Japan as Zen) with Shinto beliefs and with fighting skill.

So effective was this blend that the warrior priests were held in very high esteem throughout Japan. They stood out as persons who followed their convictions and were willing to fight to the end for what they believed. Their Zen Buddhism was based on the belief that a person must move with his or her inner feelings and not be blocked by pressures such as worry, anxiety, or fear of failure.

The warrior priests further believed that death should not be feared but rather accepted as a natural stage of existence. To die for a proper purpose was right and noble. These warriors were so fearless and successful when they went into battle that the samurai began to study the priests' beliefs and follow their actions. By the 14th century, the samurai, who had now become a separate class with special status, had absorbed many of the warrior priests into their class and had accepted their beliefs. The blending of the two traditions gave the typical Japanese warrior complexity and versatility.

Although members of the samurai class generally agreed that warriors should be courteous, loyal, benevolent, and willing to die for their masters, they disagreed on other matters. Numerous sects developed, each with its own fighting techniques, military tactics, and loyalties.

Besides the bushi, the samurai, and the warrior priests, another important group of warriors developed in early Japan. These were the *ninja*, the shadow warriors. Unlike the aristocratic bushi, the ninja were commoners who traced their ancestry to the inhabitants of Japan's hilly back country. The ninja probably first appeared sometime after A.D. 700, but their fighting techniques can be traced back as far as 500 to 300 B.C., long before the unification of Japan.

Ninja fighting techniques were influenced by the teachings of a special group of warrior monks, the *yamabushi*, who lived in the mountains of Japan. Traditional Japanese forms of combat—sumai, yawara, and tai-jutsu—also influenced the ninja. Not all of their influences, however, came from Japan. Many ninja tactics developed from lessons in a famous text, *The Art of War*, by the Chinese general Sun-Tzu.

The ninja method stressed concealment, or the ability to blend with nature. This "art of stealth," as it was called, along with the ninja's secrecy about their methods, caused outsiders to see the ninja as being cloaked in a mysterious aura.

Joining the ninja voluntarily was nearly impossible; to be a ninja, one generally had to be born into the profession. Each ninja family had its own secret arts, techniques, and weapons that were passed from one genera-

tion to the next. Disclosing these secrets to outsiders could mean death at the hands of one's own family. Likewise, a ninja was expected to take his or her own life if captured so that he or she could not be made to give up secrets.

The ninja cleverly blended their own fighting arts with the best fighting arts of Japan and were quite skilled with bow and arrow and sword. They became most famous, however, for their unique ability to use less conventional weapons. They developed special weapons, such as blow guns, hooks, spikes, brass knuckles, and an assortment of blades, darts, poisons, smoke bombs, and grenades.

Modern martial-arts experts marvel at the ninja's knowledge of chemistry and explosives. More impressive still was their use of camouflage to survive outdoors. Their greatest weapons were their intelligence, ingenuity, and ability to adapt to any challenge that faced them.

A skilled ninja had astounding muscle control and range of movement in his or her practice of "the body art." The ninja's form of tai-jutsu put special emphasis on attacks against sensitive areas of the human body.

They also developed a form of psychology for dealing with an enemy's emotions. The ninja's psychological tools included hypnosis and sleight of hand to confuse and disorient an opponent. Because their arts were kept secret from the outside world, an air of mystery has always surrounded the ninja.

The ninja became famous for fighting effectively, armed or unarmed, against any opponent, no matter what the adversary's training. Consequently, the ninja's services were in constant demand—sometimes openly, and sometimes as secret agents. They were often hired for spying, sabotage, assassination, and very difficult commando missions. Their ability to slip through enemy lines or into armed castles made them especially useful to nobles who were at war with their neighbors.

So incredible were their deeds that the ninja came to be thought of as being more than ordinary humans. They were often hired by the bushi or the wealthy to assist them in their intrigues. One daimyo wishing to gain advantage over another would probably hire ninja in addition to samurai. Because the samurai were honor-bound to follow their code and were expected to fight openly against a foe, they were not ideal for certain missions.

Ninjas were the masters of espionage, subversion, and destruction of enemy defenses. Over time, large family groups of ninja specialized in certain tasks that they would perform for the highest bidder. At times they assisted fighting monks who were battling the forces of the emperor and the rising military class of samurai.

A new period in Japanese history, the Tokugawa era, began when a strong leader, Ieyasu, became shogun in 1603. As Ieyasu attempted to end the warfare among the daimyo, he placed strict regulations on the activities of the samurai and ninja. These restrictions led to a gradual decline in the use of samurai and ninja in warfare. Despite the official suppression of the ninja, the imperial court continued to use the ninja secretly for missions that could not be carried out openly by ordinary servants.

Although the samurai no longer took part in large-scale warfare, they continued to take pride in bushi ideals and fighting forms. The samurai no longer needed to be constantly ready for battle, but the study of martial arts went on. Because of the many techniques explored during this period, the Tokugawa era can be seen as a golden age in the development of unarmed combat.

Increasingly, the term *ju-jutsu,* meaning "gentle art," was used to refer to hand-to-hand fighting systems that redirected an opponent's energy and momentum against him or her. This system included punches, strikes, kicks, holds, locks, throws, and grappling techniques, but it also reserved a place for weaponry.

People who were not samurai, however, became interested in learning the combat techniques of ju-jutsu, and eventually a second form of the art developed. The new form played down the use of weapons, punches, and kicks and was more oriented toward throws, holds, locks, and general grappling. This type of ju-jutsu is practiced for physical fitness and ordinary self-defense, not for open warfare, and is referred to as civilian ju-jutsu. The earlier type, with its life-endangering aspects, is called combat ju-jutsu. The ideals of civilian ju-jutsu were highly respected and became known as *bushido,* or "the way of the warrior."

During the Tokugawa era, another martial art, known as *kempo* (meaning "fist way"), became increasingly popular. Kempo blended Chinese fighting techniques and traditional Japanese forms of grappling. The resulting art was extremely effective and has continued to grow in popularity.

In the 19th century, European influence

became more important in the everyday affairs of Japan. Many of the samurai grew worried that their country was being spoiled. War finally broke out in the 1860s between the forces of several daimyo who wanted to keep their homeland free from outsiders and those of the shogun, who had allowed Western influence. The shogun's followers were defeated, and the Tokugawa era ended. All of the shogun's powers were transferred back to the emperor, and a new era, called the Meiji Restoration, began.

Sweeping changes took place. The class system was simplified, Japanese people gained more freedom to choose which career to pursue, agricultural policy was reformed, and the importance of the traditional samurai decreased. A law passed in the 1870s banned the wearing of swords except by military personnel. Since even a common person could be in the army, the samurai's exclusive power to wage war was gone. The popularity of fighting arts waned.

Then, a man named Jigoro Kano took the techniques of ju-jutsu that he believed could be safely practiced and created the sport of *judo,* meaning "gentle way." He aimed to keep Japan's effective fighting techniques alive by encouraging people to use them for better health. Other martial arts were similarly developed to show people the advantages of studying the techniques and tactics of Japanese self-defense.

The newer fighting arts increasingly changed the emphasis from the defeat of an enemy in a life-or-death struggle to the conquest of one's own weaknesses, such as fear, anxiety, lack of confidence, and poor health. Many of these forms of fighting, like judo, grew into arts that could also be used for sport and recreation. The study of practical fighting techniques was not lost but preserved—sometimes even enhanced—in the development of these martial-arts forms.

The lessons of the great Japanese masters are now available to interested people throughout the world. Perhaps more people than ever before are able to benefit from a concentrated study of the teachings of the ancient Japanese masters of self-defense.

3

JAPANESE PHILOSOPHY OF MARTIAL ARTS

Many of the major Japanese fighting systems are based on a philosophy, developed by Japanese masters of self-defense, that blends Shintoism, Zen Buddhism, and Confucianism.

The masters of Japanese martial arts consider people to be only one part of nature, a part that must interact with the other parts in order to be effective. Japanese *budo,* which means "way of fighting" or "martial way," advises people to accept both calm and storm, because life is continually changing.

Obstacles must be expected and overcome to reach one's goal. Many obstacles, however, are merely illusions that we create in our minds. Japanese masters have referred to these obstacles as inner dragons that must be slain before one can move ahead. Budo teaches the student to slay the dragons of fear and anxiety with understanding and full use of natural abilities. To the Japanese masters, dangerous illusions are numerous and changeable, but budo offers a tool for facing and overcoming them. Once this inner discipline has been learned, students can more easily handle obvious external difficulties that confront them at school, on the job, or in other situations of possible conflict.

Budo teaches that people must learn to understand themselves and their abilities. If they use their natural abilities, they can create harmony. To act in harmony with nature's rules is a major goal taught by many of the Japanese masters. Physical force is only to be used to return to a balanced harmony, not to destroy harmony. The following are 12 basic martial-arts principles emphasized by the Japanese masters.

1. Jiko no Kansei

The principle of *jiko no kansei* holds that one should strive for perfection of character. The Japanese masters taught that nature is constantly evolving, and people, like plants, either grow or begin to die. The value of this effort is in the striving for perfection, not in the actual achievement of it. No student is expected to be truly perfect, but every student must continually work toward being a complete person.

Each of the Japanese fighting arts has its own way of striving for perfection, but they share the belief that martial arts practitioners, through continual work toward perfection, will achieve both inner and outer harmony by breaking through psychological barriers. Practitioners who make progress in slaying their inner dragons will more successfully harmonize with others and find more than the ability to defend themselves. They will achieve self-esteem.

2. Bunbu-ichi or Bunbu-Ryodo

The concept of *bunbu-ichi,* or *bunbu-ryodo,* is usually translated as "the pen and sword in accord." Masters of the Japanese martial arts emphasize the development of a balanced personality in which an interest in literature and the arts, symbolized by the pen, combines with the martial spirit and skill, symbolized by the sword.

Budo requires of students not only steadiness of spirit but also learning and harmony. According to one often-told story, a cowardly warrior who wanted to improve his effectiveness in battle was shocked when his superiors ordered him to study the ways of a successful businessperson. As he observed the obstacles that the businessperson faced, however, the warrior was impressed by the steady, consistent resolve with which the businessperson overcame them. The next time he faced battle, the warrior tried to imitate the businessperson's spirit and found himself a fearless fighter drawing new effectiveness from this unusual training session. In telling this story, the Japanese masters intended to cultivate an attitude that would give students the spirit to be successful in all pursuits and make them well-rounded people.

3. Mushin

Mushin means "no mind" and refers to a state in which no mental obstacles stand in the way of action. The Japanese masters have long known that self-consciousness can be a serious obstacle to success. You can easily illustrate this concept by performing some ordinary, everyday action and consciously examining yourself as you do it. If you concentrate on your feet while you walk down steps, you will falter. Effectiveness is gained, however, if you can think beyond the small details of what you must do, move spontaneously, and proceed toward your goal.

4. Mizu no Kokoro

The expression *mizu no kokoro* means "mind like water." When a body of water is calm and clear, it will reflect everything around it, much like a mirror. A martial-arts practitioner should keep his or her mind free of anxiety. A calm mind can take in all of the surroundings, including any potential dangers, and focus on the real opponent.

5. Tsuki no Kokoro

The expression *tsuki no kokoro,* meaning "mind like the moon," refers to the ability not only to take in everything but to do so without distorting anything. The sun shines brightly and casts dark shadows that may conceal some objects. The moon, however, shines more softly, giving light without deep shadows. The defender in a conflict should see everything and not concentrate on just one part of the attacker's body. Similarly, the Japanese masters teach that in any confrontation, success depends on accurately evaluating all of the elements involved.

6. Hara

The *hara* is a person's center of gravity. The Japanese masters believed that great power is derived from centering the spirit in the proper place in the body, about two inches below the navel. Training develops concentration that can bring energy from this center out to the part of the body being used. This centering not only promotes greater power and stability but also eliminates stress.

7. Kime

The ability to use *kime,* which means "focus," is a great instrument for harnessing a person's natural force. Many people scatter their vital energy and enthusiasm among too many projects. As a result, very little is achieved and the spirit becomes splintered. When people focus all of their attention on one purpose, they not only bring more power to bear but leave no room for fear.

Someone who is extremely well focused while executing a martial-arts technique can seem to have almost supernatural power. Proper focus can lead to more power and greater effectiveness in many nonmartial pursuits as well.

8. Suki

During *suki,* "the gap between action," people are vulnerable because their attention and strength may be low. This phenomenon has been recognized by the Japanese masters for centuries, and training has therefore concentrated on eliminating any unnecessary time between actions. Observing gaps between an aggressor's actions and exploiting them by attacking during that weak time is also important.

In self-defense, any blow, hold, or throwing technique should be timed to take advantage of an opponent's suki. Likewise, in ordinary living, those people who recognize a suki or opportunity and move quickly can often gain a tremendous advantage.

9. Seiryoku Zenryo

The average person wastes a great deal of energy. How often at the end of the day have you heard someone say, "I'm exhausted, yet I didn't really get anything done"? Japanese budo understands that progress toward a goal is not always directly proportional to the effort spent on it. The concept of *seiryoku zenryo,* which means "maximum efficiency with minimum effort," teaches how to achieve a goal while retaining energy to do other things.

If an aggressor attacks, use that person's own strength against him or her. Do not directly oppose an aggressor, but redirect the energy of the attack. By doing this, you conserve your own energy and use the attacker's momentum against him or her. For example, if an aggressor pushes you backward, do not try to regain your original position so that you can then push him or her backward. Instead, pull the aggressor forward in the same direction he or she pushed you. The aggressor will be thrown off balance and most of the energy used will be your opponent's, not yours.

This principle of the budo is used in ju-jutsu by small persons to throw very powerful attackers. It allows a person to remain relaxed and full of power so that a great deal of energy can be summoned when needed.

Anxiety, guilt, or frustration use up energy that could be much better used. The concept of seiryoku zenryo suggests that you recognize these emotions but not waste energy on them. Instead, use the energy brought out by them to accomplish something.

10. Kufu

The Japanese masters recognized that roadblocks of one kind or another hinder everyone's progress. The successful person must remember the principle of *kufu,* which holds that one should not give up struggling until released. Persistence will lead to victory. This willingness to wrestle with a problem until it is solved is the trademark of a successful person in the martial arts, business, or any other field.

11. Kyo-jutsu Tenkan Ho

Defeating a skilled opponent in a fight or any other competition may depend on taking advantage of the way the other person perceives the situation. If an adversary's perception is incorrect, he or she may leave an opening for an attack. You can use the concept of *kyo-jutsu tenkan ho,* which means "delivering falsehood as truth," to make openings that you can use against an aggressor. By using fakes or deceptive tactics, you can confuse an opponent. If, for example, you throw a punch in one direction to force a block by an opponent, you can strike with the other hand at an opening elsewhere on the opponent's body. It is also valuable to be aware that an opponent may be attempting to use kyo-jutsu tenkan ho.

Never present falsehood as truth unless the goal is ethically and morally correct. Sometimes, presenting a falsehood as reality does no unnecessary harm and allows you to defend yourself successfully. At other times, however, using kyo-jutsu tenkan ho may be an improper way of taking advantage of someone. Keep in mind that the principle was intended by the ancient Japanese masters only for use against a dangerous enemy. Each individual must choose whether and when he or she is comfortable using it.

12. Bushido

Most modern Japanese systems teach that students should follow the ethical code known as *bushido*, which means "the way of the warrior." Bushido is based on ancient samurai rules of conduct followed for many centuries and finally put into a written code in more modern times. It requires that a martial artist practice the following virtues:

- **Loyalty**—Warriors must show loyalty to their superiors and be willing to follow them in difficult times.
- **Justice**—Warriors must see that others are treated fairly and must not act unfairly.
- **Courage**—Warriors must move forward without thought of retreat. Courage must be shown even in the face of death.
- **Benevolence**—To be complete, warriors must show love, affection, and sympathy for other human beings.
- **Politeness**—Proper manners and general courtesy must be used in dealings with other people. In this way, warriors show that they have no fear or insecurity.
- **Truthfulness**—Lying is dishonorable. A warrior's word must be reliable.
- **Honor**—A warrior's honor and reputation must be upheld in everything. He or she must be willing to sacrifice to protect both personal and family honor.

CHAPTER

4

COMMON QUESTIONS

1. What does it mean to practice shin-jutsu?

Shin-jutsu means "the skills of the mind and heart." Many times the word *heart* is used interchangeably with the word *spirit* by martial artists. One of the common themes that runs through the lessons of the various Japanese masters is the importance of bringing together the mind, spirit, and body into one unified force for effective living. People who practice shin-jutsu are able to unify their natural forces to accomplish any goal. It is a very high compliment to be said to practice shin-jutsu.

2. What are containment techniques?

The essence of good self-defense is to avoid harm while doing the least amount of damage to an opponent. Containment techniques end an attacker's aggression by making him or her unable to move against the defender. Examples of such techniques are holds or locks, which are more often used against joints or sensitive areas on the body. A strong attacker has often been defeated by the application of a timely arm bar or wrist lock.

3. What did the warrior priests contribute to the martial arts?

More than one group of warrior priests originated in Japan. One group that had an especially effective fighting style combined

Zen Buddhism, Shinto beliefs, certain Chinese fighting techniques, traditional Japanese hand-to-hand fighting, and the use of weapons. These warrior priests contributed not only to the development of bu-jutsu (which means "martial arts") but also to an understanding of life. They taught that one should meet challenges head-on without thought of winning or losing, that one should not fear the future or the possibility of death, and that one must learn to live one day at a time. This philosophy freed warriors from the mental distractions that might diminish their fighting effectiveness and their ability to appreciate the present.

4. What did ninja warriors contribute to the martial arts?

Ninja warriors employed a variety of specialized weapons, including blow guns, swords, collapsible bows, knives, hooks, brass knuckles, spikes, and flying darts. Ninja training classes are still being offered today. Each school has its own individual techniques and emphasizes certain weapons.

5. How do you suggest I start my training in self-defense?

Before starting any self-defense training, you should have a full medical exam to see if any health problems would interfere with your ability to train in the martial arts. Any exam should include not only a general checkup but also an assessment of the flexibility of your ankles, knees, and wrists—all of which are used extensively in martial-arts training. People who are in good health but not in excellent physical condition should, at a minimum, go through an elementary physical-conditioning program before starting self-defense classes. Only a body that is strong and flexible can efficiently handle martial-arts training.

If you are in excellent physical condition, then investigate a variety of martial-arts systems by visiting schools, reading books, and talking with students of Asian fighting arts. Get a feel for the classes in your area that may meet your particular needs. Each individual is looking for certain things—peak physical efficiency, self-defense skills, or an enjoyable hobby that will allow for continued growth—in the martial arts. No matter which goal, or combination of goals, is right for you, you can probably find a martial-arts class to meet your needs.

Do not start training without first asking what will be required of you. Do not sign any long-term contracts that would require you to continue paying whether you train or not. Also consider the safety precautions taken at a particular school. Beginning students should be supervised while training and should not be rushed into sparring or free fighting without proper physical and emotional preparation. Once you find a school that meets your needs, work diligently on your training. You may want to quit at times, but persistence through those difficult periods will bring tremendous rewards.

CHAPTER
5

CONDITIONING

When the body is supple, strong, and properly conditioned, fighting techniques come much more easily. Even if you never have to use your self-defense skills, a properly conditioned body will make you look and feel healthier. Once the conditioning process stops, however, the body begins to decline. For that reason, you should establish an enjoyable conditioning routine that will become a lifelong habit.

Before starting any exercise program, have a full medical checkup. Discuss thoroughly with your doctor whether any limitations should be put on your training, and ask specifically whether you would have a problem doing any stretching exercises that involve the ankles, knees, or wrists.

If your doctor approves a conditioning program, do not expect to jump in and attempt an overall body-building regimen. Instead, begin with a few exercises and slowly build from there. The exercises in this chapter are only the basics for starting the conditioning process.

STRETCHING EXERCISES

Stretch for at least 20 minutes three times a week to develop a supple body. Perform stretches very slowly. Hold the stretch at its farthest point for a count of at least five seconds to get a release of tension, but never force any action or push the body beyond a natural stopping point. Exercise should not be painful; if an exercise hurts, stop doing it immediately. If your body becomes sore after an exercise session, give yourself a rest in order to recover. Rest is just as important as exercise in building physical fitness. At first, exercise your joints, such as your wrists or ankles, only under the supervision of a qualified instructor.

In each exercise described below, remember to stretch slowly, smoothly, and only as far as you can without feeling strain. You should also use an exercise mat to cover the floor—especially for those exercises that require you to lie down.

Neck Stretch

Stand erect with your feet slightly apart and your arms hanging loosely at your sides. Drop your chin gently toward your chest; then return to the starting point. Repeat this procedure four more times.

Being careful not to stretch beyond your body's natural stopping point, turn your head slowly to the left as if looking behind you; then return to the starting position. Repeat four more times to the left, and then perform the same turning action to the right for five repetitions.

Next, tip your head toward your left shoulder. Let your head move down naturally; then return to the starting position. Repeat four more times to the left and then do the same to your right five times.

Hamstring Stretch

Stand erect with your feet close together, knees slightly bent, and arms hanging loosely at your sides. Reach your arms up above your head. Slowly bring your arms down toward the ground. Go only as far as is comfortable; do not force the action or bounce up and down. This exercise must be performed gradually in order to accomplish the necessary stretch. Return to the starting position and repeat the exercise at least four more times.

Basic Sit-up

Lie on your back on the floor, bend your knees, and place the soles of your feet flat on the floor. Bring your head up so that your chin is tucked in toward your chest. Then reach your arms forward as you sit up. Move forward only as far as you can without feeling any strain. Your hands will probably reach your knees. Return to the beginning position on the floor. Try to do at least five sit-ups each session.

Basic One-Leg Back Stretch on the Ground

Lie on your back with your knees bent. Put your hands behind your left thigh near the knee and bring your left leg as close to your chest as you comfortably can. Do not pull hard or bounce while stretching, but go slowly and gradually. Return to your original position. Repeat this procedure with the same leg four more times, and then do the same stretch five times with your right leg.

Basic Body Stretch on the Ground

Lie on your back with your knees bent and your feet flat on the floor. Bring your chin toward your chest. Next, reach both hands behind your bent legs and bring your knees up toward your chest. Take them only as far as is comfortable, then return to the original position. Repeat four times.

Basic Side Stretch

Stand erect with your feet spread apart to about shoulder width. Place your left hand on your hip and reach your bent right arm over your head as far to the left as you comfortably can. Stand up straight and do a similar stretch to the right. Stretch at least three times to each side of the body.

Body Twist

Stand with your feet apart at shoulder width, your knees slightly bent, and your arms (bent at the elbow) at chest level. Step back with your right foot while twisting at the waist to the right as far as you can comfortably go. Then do the same stretch to the left. Stretch in each direction at least three times.

Basic Two-Leg Stretch

Stand erect with your feet spread slightly apart. Slowly spread your legs as far apart as possible without straining the muscles. Do not bounce while stretching. Once you have reached the lowest position you can attain without strain, hold for a count of five. This exercise must be done gradually so that the legs can develop flexibility without injury. Perform this exercise only once during any training session.

Basic Lower-Leg Stretch

Place the palms of your hands against the shoulder of a practice partner, a wall, or some other solid object and move your feet back at least three feet away. Bend your elbows to bring your chest closer to the person or object. Hold that position for a count of at least 10.

Basic Wrist Stretch

NOTE: Before starting any wrist-stretching program, consult with your doctor. Beginners should first perform any wrist-stretching exercise only under the supervision of a qualified instructor. The wrist is a sensitive joint that should never be put under any great strain. If you have arthritis, a history of injury to the joint, or any other condition that weakens or stiffens the joints, do not practice joint locks. A basic exercise routine for most people who have received a doctor's approval for wrist exercise may be similar to the following.

To perform the wrist circle, slowly and gently roll your wrist in a circle while bending your hand back only as far as you can without pain or discomfort. Rotate each wrist first in one direction and then in the other. The wrist should become loose and pliable so that it is not easily injured in practice. Never force any wrist action. Immediately stop exercising if you experience any discomfort.

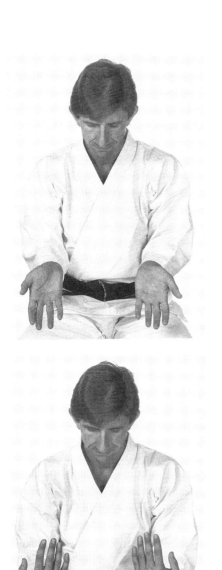

Arm and Shoulder Stretches

Grasp a towel at both ends. Slip it behind your back, and hold it vertically with the top end just behind your head. Bring the top half down as far as possible, and then draw the bottom of the towel up as far as you can. Repeat the two-way stretch two more times. Then reverse hand positions on the towel and do the same exercise three times.

27

Two-Arm Rear Stretch

Stand between two practice partners or in front of an open doorway. Reach behind you and grab your partners' shoulders or both sides of the door frame. Hold with your arms in a nearly straight position for a count of 10.

Ankle Conditioners

NOTE: If you have stiff ankles or a history of ankle pain or injury, ask your doctor which exercises, if any, you can do without risking damage to the joint. If your doctor approves an exercise program, follow it carefully and exercise under the supervision of a qualified trainer. The ankle stretches in your program may be similar to those that follow.

Sit with your knees bent so that your feet comfortably touch the ground but do not bear any of your weight. Turn your ankles gently inward only as far as is comfortable and hold the position for a count of five. Relax and repeat the process three more times. Next, slowly turn your ankles outward and hold for a count of five. Relax and repeat the process three more times. Do not force any action or bounce with the stretching motion. Instead, allow your ankles to move slowly and gently as far as they naturally can. Next, turn your toes downward and hold for a count of five; then relax and repeat the process one more time. Turn your toes upward as far as they can go without forcing and hold for a count of five, then relax. Repeat once. With each foot, do toe stretches upward and downward twice.

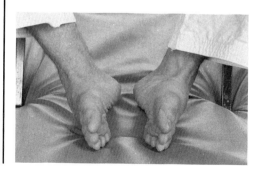

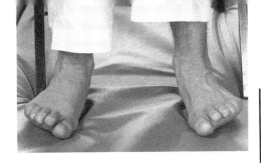

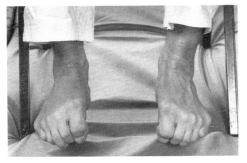

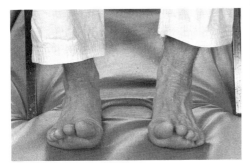

lower body. When these exercises become easy, increase the repetitions or try additional exercises, keeping in mind your overall conditioning goal of flexibility and strength.

Leg Conditioner

The foundation of a strong defense is leg power. To develop upper-leg power, stand with your back to a wall. Bend your knees about halfway, as though you were starting to sit down in a chair. Hold that position for a count of 25, and then stand straight. This exercise should be done only once in each exercise session. You should gradually increase the length of time that you can hold this bent-knee position.

STRENGTHENING EXERCISES

There are many ways to strengthen the body and tone muscles. Be careful, however, not to sacrifice flexibility and endurance as you build strength. A combination of strength and flexibility will make you feel healthy without the restriction caused by overemphasis on muscle tone. The simple exercises that follow will strengthen both the upper and

Push-up

This exercise builds the upper body, especially the chest, upper back, and arms. Put the palms of your hands on the ground while maintaining balance on your toes, and lower yourself until your chest almost touches the floor. Push yourself up, keeping your head straight. Do not lock your arms completely straight when moving to an upward position, and do not let your arms be in an overly bent position when your chest is at its lowest point. Raise and lower yourself five times.

Basic Wrist, Hand, and Forearm Conditioner

Hold a small rubber ball in the palm of your hand. Squeeze the ball for a count of two, and then release it. Do at least three squeezes with each hand. Gradually build up until you can squeeze the ball at least five times with each hand.

AEROBIC EXERCISES

To succeed in the martial arts, you need not only power, flexibility, and coordination but also the endurance to sustain a technique after prolonged, extreme physical exertion. To do this you must have the proper cardiovascular conditioning.

Running, swimming, bicycling, and walking are all good aerobic exercises. These are exercises that improve cardiovascular fitness. Pick a conditioning exercise and perform it at least three times a week to build endurance. You will find that it also provides an enjoyable escape from everyday pressures. If you have problems with your knees or ankles, you should avoid exercises (such as running) that put stress on the joints. Concentrate instead on swimming, bicycling, or walking. After your doctor approves, start slowly with any aerobic exercise to see if you enjoy it.

Running

Running builds not only endurance but also overall body strength. Start slowly and increase your distance and speed gradually. Be careful to pick a flat course and wear the proper running shoes to lessen the impact of each footfall on your joints. You do not have to become a marathon runner to have adequate endurance for self-defense. Normally, a three-mile run three times a week is sufficient for proper conditioning.

Swimming

Swimming can be enjoyable, relaxing, and effective as a body conditioner. Emphasize endurance, rather than a leisurely pace, while swimming. Do a number of laps in a pool or some other small area of water.

Bicycling

Riding a bicycle can be an excellent way to develop your leg muscles and gain overall endurance. For maximum conditioning, pick the proper bicycle height and adjust your bike to your size. A beginner will probably find that a multi-speed bicycle is best. Stronger riders, however, may find great enjoyment in riding an older, single-speed bicycle that requires more effort.

Walking

As the Japanese masters have long known, a brisk walk for about 30 minutes every day is an excellent form of aerobic exercise. To get extra walking time, try walking as a form of transportation, instead of taking a bus, subway, taxi, or car.

FALLING EXERCISES

The ancient Japanese masters realized that to minimize the risk of injury, a student of self-defense must learn how to fall correctly. A person who knows how to fall correctly also will gain confidence by losing his or her fear of being thrown. At first, do falling exercises only under the supervision of a qualified instructor. Also, always observe the following guidelines:

1. Always practice on a large, thick mat designed for judo or ju-jutsu practice. Never practice on a hard surface.
2. Always warm up before practice with at least 20 minutes of stretching exercises to make your body flexible.
3. Perform each falling technique slowly at first. Do not speed up until you have mastered the proper form of the technique.
4. Do not allow anyone to throw you until your falling skills are excellent and until a qualified instructor gives permission for you to be thrown. Even after such permission is granted, an instructor should be present when you are learning how to react to being thrown by a partner.
5. Never throw a partner in practice unless that person has excellent falling skills and has permission from your instructor to be thrown. When executing a throw, do it slowly and gently, carefully guiding your partner to the mat. Do everything possible to safeguard against injury to him or her.
6. Don't become careless during practice. Pay attention to what you are doing and stay loose and flexible during falling exercises.

Side Fall

This frequently used falling technique is especially effective when you are thrown over an opponent's hip, shoulder, or leg. To practice it, begin in a squatting position with one leg crossed in front of the other. Keep your chin tucked down so that your head never hits the mat. Gradually slide your front leg forward so that you lose balance and fall to one side.

While falling, raise the arm that is nearer to the mat. Just before your body hits the mat, slap the palm of your raised hand against the mat to break your fall. Your body should land in such a way that your knees, ankles, and other sensitive areas are not hurt.

Rear Fall

This falling technique is useful when you fall or are thrown backward. To practice it, get into a squatting position with your knees bent. Tuck in your chin and extend your arms directly in front of you. Spring up with your knees and allow your body to fall backward. As you fall, extend an arm out to each side of your body. Just before your back hits the mat, slap your forearms down against the mat to break your fall. Your head should not touch the mat at any point during the fall.

Roll Fall

This technique allows you to fall forward without harming the vital parts of your body. To practice it, begin in a kneeling position on the mat. Tuck your chin toward your chest and slide one arm out to the side as you turn over in a somersault. Slap the palm of your outstretched hand against the mat to break your fall just before you land. After you become accustomed to this roll fall, you can try continuing forward out of the roll and up into a standing position.

facing the mat. Slap the mat with the palms of both hands to break your fall. Your head and abdomen should not touch the mat at any time. Keep your hands and arms stationary after they slap the mat so they can support your body and keep it from hitting the mat.

Front Fall

The front fall can be effective when someone tackles, sweeps, or throws you forward. It can also be used whenever you slip and fall forward. To practice it, begin by squatting until you can put your knees on the mat—so that your body is supported by your knees and the bottoms of your flexed toes. Rise up on your toes and let your body fall forward. Bring your arms up with the palms of your hands

C H A P T E R

6

POSTURE
AND MOVEMENT

Body positioning and movement contribute to a proper foundation for defense. Beginning students should first practice the basic stances for self-defense and then work at moving from one stance to another. Movement itself can be a defense, and switching from one stance to another is sometimes very effective against an adversary. After all, the strongest blow by an opponent will amount to nothing if you can evade its force.

Besides practicing your techniques in front of a qualified instructor who can help you correct your form and movement, you should use a mirror when practicing alone to help you correct any problems on your own. Compare your form with the photographs in this chapter to make sure you are performing the techniques correctly. Practice each stance using all three basic types of hand-guard positions.

STANCES

Natural Stance

The natural stance is a starting position that simulates a natural standing position. It can be used in many situations—such as the start of a holding or throwing technique—and is comfortable enough to maintain for a long time. Stand erect with your feet approximately 2 to 10 inches apart. Relax your shoulders and let your arms hang comfortably in front of you or at your sides. Focus your eyes directly forward on your opponent while your back remains straight.

To assume a right natural stance, simply start in the natural stance and then move your right foot forward so that you are facing your opponent diagonally. For a left natural stance, do the same but with your left foot. In any natural stance, face forward and distribute your weight equally on both feet.

Forward Stance

The samurai's respect for front-facing stances is reflected in one of their sayings: "Test your armor, but only test the front." The samurai often assumed a forward battle stance—a confident, assertive self-defense position that expresses a positive attitude.

This stance begins with your left foot one and one half to two shoulder widths in front of and to the side of your right foot. Bend your left (forward) leg and place most of your weight on it. Your hands may be in the mid-guard position described later in this chapter.

Back Stance

This stance is excellent for defense. To assume the back stance, place one leg in front of the other so that your feet are one and a half to two shoulder widths apart. Bend your front leg only slightly, but keep your rear leg deeply bent and let it carry about 70 percent of your weight. Your hands may be in the mid-guard position.

Horse Stance

To assume this versatile stance, stand with your feet one and a half to two shoulder widths apart, as if you were straddling a horse. Keep your torso erect and your weight evenly distributed over your legs.

Variations of this stance are the diagonal and side-facing horse stances. In the diagonal horse stance, you place one foot forward and turn the top half of your body toward your opponent. In contrast, the side-facing horse stance places just one side of your body in line with your opponent.

In any horse stance, your hands may be fisted, palms facing up. Although in practice sessions your fists are usually kept above your hips, in a real confrontation you should use whichever hand-guard position offers the best defense.

HAND POSITIONS

The three basic hand positions—low guard, mid guard, and high guard—can be held in any of the stances. One way to confuse an adversary is to change hand positions while you are moving. As the following guidelines show, your choice of a particular hand guard will depend on your purposes, your distance from your opponent, and other aspects of the fighting situation.

Low Guard

Make fists with both hands and hold them approximately at hip level. To protect your ribs, keep your elbows against them. While in a low-guard position, your hands are ready to protect your groin and lower abdomen but are still available for throwing very quick punches. A low guard may be appropriate when you are at long range from an opponent. Long range is a distance from which your lower body may be easier for your opponent to hit.

Mid Guard

Hold both hands approximately at chest level with the palms open and facing outward. At times you may need to make both hands into fists. You may occasionally need to make one hand into a fist, while keeping the other hand open for blocking and grabbing. The mid-guard position allows you to move quickly to protect your head or your lower body. It is especially useful when you are quite close to an aggressor. In the mid-guard position, your hands can parry attacks, launch open-hand blows, punch, or grab an aggressor's body.

High Guard

Hold your elbows against your ribs, with your fists at approximately shoulder level. Protect your chin by dropping it toward your chest. This position is excellent for quick hand maneuvers, and it lets you protect your upper body. The high guard is especially useful against a high kicking or punching attack and for close-range fighting, when your head and chest are easy for your opponent to hit.

MOVEMENT

Pivoting Evasion

In this type of movement, you evade an attack by pivoting on your forward foot. It is most often used from a forward stance or diagonal horse stance. To begin, pivot on your front foot and swing the rear of your body in the desired direction. After pivoting, make sure that the rear foot is planted firmly on the ground again. At the end of the movement, you should be in a strong fighting stance and ready for action.

Single Step

You can use a single step to move forward or backward from any fighting stance. Maintain your balance while stepping, and keep your upper body erect. When moving ahead from a basic natural stance, step forward and to the side with the foot that you want in front. At the end of the movement you will be in a diagonal horse stance.

ward to the desired position. Keep your other foot solidly on the ground. To protect your groin, avoid making any wide swings with the leg that is moving. To use the stepping movement backward, simply reverse the procedure.

Stepping

Stepping is a movement you can use to change which side of your body is forward—for example, to move from a left-facing diagonal horse stance to the same stance with the right side forward. Begin by barely lifting one foot off the ground and by bringing it for-

Slide Step

Start in a front stance, a side-facing horse stance, or a diagonal horse stance. Slide your front foot forward. Next, slide your rear foot forward until you have regained your original stance. Maintain proper balance as you move. To go backward, slide your rear foot backward, then follow with your front foot.

2

1

3

Side Step

You can begin this movement, which is useful for evading many different attacks, with either your front or rear foot. To lead off with your front foot, start in a fighting stance such as a diagonal horse stance. Step to the side with your front foot, and then slide your rear foot toward it. Turn your hips, if necessary, to keep your body outside of the line of your opponent's attack. At the same time, keep your hands ready to protect against any blows that you cannot evade. Adjust the length of your step so that even if the attack misses, you stay in range to counterattack.

When beginning with your rear foot, first step diagonally out with that foot and then follow by moving your front foot to the rear. Keep your hands ready to block while you twist your hips to bring your body out of the line of attack.

2

1

3

Circle Movement

Besides helping you evade an attack, the circle movement lets you maintain your body position while moving around the attacker. Move your forward foot 4 to 8 inches in the direction you want to move. Once your advancing foot has moved into place, use it as a pivot to swing the rest of the body in the desired direction. After this two-step move, your rear foot should be planted firmly on the ground and you should again be in a strong fighting stance.

1   2

3

Unbalancing Movement

Sometimes your opponent's own actions, such as changing body position, may make him or her vulnerable to being thrown off balance. If you can take advantage of these situations, you may be able to prevent an attack or begin to perform a takedown. The Japanese call unbalancing movements, in which you use an opponent's own actions against him or her, *kuzushi*. For example, when an aggressor pushes you backward, you can use that motion to throw him or her off balance by pulling in that direction. You could also pivot to turn your body to the side and throw him or her off balance. If an aggressor pulls you forward, you could take advantage of that motion either by pushing him or her or by moving your body toward him or her in a way that puts your opponent off balance.

The key to each of these unbalancing techniques is to use the aggressor's own strength and energy against him or her instead of directly opposing it. It is especially important that an aggressor's balance be broken before you try to accomplish any throw. When a person is put off balance, most of his or her weight is moving in one direction, and you can more easily throw him or her in that direction.

Balance is also affected by the direction in which a person's head is bent. For example, when an aggressor's head is bent forward, it is easier to throw that person in that direction. By observing and taking advantage of an aggressor's balance problems, you may be able to out-maneuver and throw even a heavier, stronger person.

You may respond to the move in photograph No. 1 with the moves in photographs No. 2 or No. 3.

3

1

2

You may respond to the move in photograph No. 4 with the moves in photographs No. 5 or No. 6.

4

6

5

CHAPTER
7
SENSITIVE AREAS
OF THE BODY

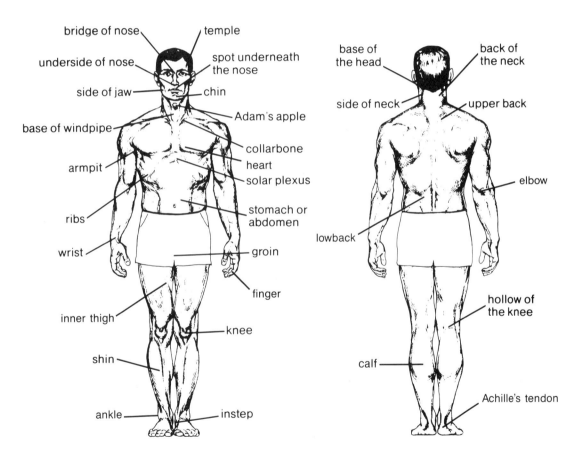

Sometimes simple evasion will not stop an attacker. You may have to exert force against a sensitive area on the opponent's body to end a fight. Japanese masters called the practice of hitting these sensitive areas *atemi-waza*.

The charts in this chapter show sensitive areas of the front and back of the body. Slight or moderate pressure on some of these areas can cause significant pain. For example, by bending an opponent's small finger backward, you can cause great pain. To other, stronger areas of the body, a forceful blow might cause enough pain to end the fight. One such area is the stomach. A well-placed punch there can take the fight out of even a very powerful person.

In many fights, each person hits his or her opponent several times before the fight ends. This waste of energy—and the risk of injury it brings—is highly unnecessary. Martial-arts students can end many confrontations quickly by learning to hit, press, bend, or even pinch the sensitive areas shown in this chapter. Even if it is necessary to hit an area more than once, or two different areas in quick succession, a fight might still be much shorter than if the sensitive areas were ignored.

When you practice, however, *do not* use pressure or force on a partner's sensitive areas. Instead, simply learn to locate these areas and slowly simulate techniques in their direction without actually making contact. Avoid even simulating attacks against certain sensitive areas that are easily injured, such as the eyes, nose, Adam's apple, groin, and knees.

All practice of atemi techniques should be done only under the supervision of a qualified instructor. You should release your techniques with force only on a punching bag or other similar device. Keep in mind that sensitive areas should be attacked only when you are in actual danger of physical harm in a real confrontation.

8

BASIC DEFENSE AND COUNTERATTACKS WHILE STANDING

As you learn to be flexible and react spontaneously in self-defense situations, you will begin to get a feel for the three levels of the body at which attacks are directed: the upper level (from the top of the head to the shoulders), the middle level (from the shoulders to the belt line), and the lower level (from the belt line to the feet). The basic

In determining what techniques to use in a confrontation, consider the distance between you and your adversary. There are three recognizable distances in fighting: safety range, long range, and close range. Safety range is the distance at which neither you nor your opponent can reach each other with a blow. At long range, your kicks and some longer punches may reach your opponent—and his or hers may reach you. At close range, you and your opponent will be able to hit each other with strikes—circular, palm-up, or short straight punches. You may also be near enough to grab one another to apply a hold or lock, or perform a throw.

For ease of learning, the self-defense situations that follow are organized according to the range of distance between the parties when the confrontation begins. Also, unless otherwise stated, we will assume that each party's left arm and leg are forward. This is the position frequently used among combatants.

defense and counterattack techniques taught in this part of the book take each of these levels into account.

The attacker will often strike at one level and then follow through with a technique aimed at another level. You should practice combining defenses at different levels so that you can handle rapid-fire, multi-level attacks. Likewise, your own counterattacks should throw combinations of techniques at different levels to confuse your opponent.

For practical self-defense reasons, a combination of techniques is taught as part of the defense against a certain attack. Learn to combine these suggested techniques so that they flow smoothly together in a quick and effective manner. Then, try adding other techniques as you practice.

SAFETY RANGE AND LONG RANGE

Low Block and Punch against a Front Kick

When an attacker throws a front kick at your stomach, make your forward (left) hand into a fist and position it across your body. Bring the left arm down with a sweeping motion so that the outer edge of the forearm sweeps away the opponent's leg before it hits your body. After completing this block, slide forward as you release a rear-hand punch toward the mid-level of the attacker's body. Follow up with additional blows, if necessary.

Cross Block and Throw against a Front Kick

Another way to block an aggressor's kick is with a cross block. Simply cross your arms in front of you so that the kicking leg strikes the point where your arms cross. Once the attacking leg has been stopped, immediately grab the leg. You may then turn it, forcing the aggressor's body to turn away from you. You can continue to lift the leg as you push your opponent further off balance. After grabbing the attacking leg you may, instead of turning it, simply lift it up as you move your rear leg forward to a point just behind the attacker's supporting leg. Then push your opponent backward as you kick his or her supporting leg out from underneath.

Rising Block with Counterattack against a Right Punch

When an aggressor throws a right (rear) straight punch, you can deflect it with a left rising block. To counterattack, twist your right hip forward as you execute a right-hand punch, with one knuckle extended, into the attacker's solar plexus. Follow up, if necessary, by grabbing your opponent's upper arms, neutralizing them as you bring your right knee up forcefully into the groin. Then finish by stamping on your opponent's foot with your right foot.

These multi-blow counterattacks are for use against very strong attackers who would not be stopped by a single blow. You should, however, only use that amount of reasonable force necessary for self-defense. Once an attacker is immobilized, no further attacking techniques should be thrown.

Rising Block with Counterattack against a Left Jab

A punch with the forward arm is called a jab. If an aggressor moves toward you with a left jab, raise your right (rear) arm, palm facing outward, to block and deflect the attacking punch. You may counterattack by throwing your own left jab. As this blow strikes your opponent, your knuckles should be up and the palm of your hand facing down.

If your first blow is blocked or is ineffective, follow up quickly with a more powerful right-hand punch. This combination of left jab and right punch can be quite effective. It can be even better if you vary the levels of your attacks in order to confuse your opponent.

Parry with Counterattack against a Left Jab

A rising block alone is not the most effective defense if an aggressor throws a quick series of left jabs. A defense called a *parry*, however, can both deflect the first jab and keep your opponent from throwing more jabs.

When an aggressor throws a left jab, deflect it by bringing the palm of your right hand against the outside of the attacking arm, turning it inward and away. This will probably put the aggressor off balance by turning his or her body away from you. From this position, he or she cannot easily reach you with any further jabs. Immediately after completing the parry, grab the aggressor's left arm with your right hand as you make an upper-level counterattack with a left straight punch. Follow up by dropping your left hand down to grab the aggressor's left arm as your right hand shoots out with a straight punch to the head.

Parry and Ridge-Hand Strike against a Lunge Punch

If an aggressor lunges forward with the rear (right) leg as he or she launches a right straight punch, you may move forward to parry it from the inside, turning it out and away with the palm of your left hand. Bring your right hand, open with the thumb folded down into the palm, up in a circular movement and snap it inward to hit the side of your opponent's neck with the hard edge on the thumb side of your hand. (This blow is called a *ridge-hand strike.*) Follow up by driving your left fist up and under the aggressor's chin.

Parry with Arm Bar and Takedown against an Open-Hand Blow

If an attacker launches an open-hand blow with his or her left hand toward the upper level of your body, parry the attacking arm with the palm of your right hand as you step forward with your right leg. Your right parrying hand should be on the outside of the attacking arm, pushing it inward and up. Once the force of the blow has been neutralized, use your left hand to grab your opponent's left arm by the wrist and turn it palm-up. With your right hand against the back of the attacker's left elbow, pivot your body to face the same direction your opponent is facing, and lift the captured arm. Then pull up on your opponent's left wrist with your left hand as you push down on the elbow with your right hand. To finish the action, slide your right leg up against the front of the aggressor's nearer leg and kick back to knock him or her off balance.

Evasion, Parry, and Takedown against a Swinging Punch

Some aggressors like to throw wide, swinging punches, a move that may leave them off balance and vulnerable to a possible takedown. If an aggressor throws a right-hand swinging blow at you, quickly step to the left with your forward foot and then slide your rear foot toward it. (You should end up almost behind the attacker.) As you are moving, use your right hand to sweep his or her punching arm away and down from the outside. Quickly grab the punching arm with your right hand and grab some of the clothing at the rear of the aggressor's upper body with your left hand. While doing so, turn to face the same direction the attacker is facing. Next, move your right foot in between the attacker's legs. Your grip on that person's body should keep him or her from punching you. As you reach down to grab and pull back on one of your opponent's calves or ankles, drive your body close. This combination should throw him or her face-forward toward the ground.

Inward Parry, Grab, and Counterattack against a Body Punch

When an aggressor throws a right punch at your body, bring your left hand up and then inward to deflect the attacking arm. Then quickly grab the punching arm with your left hand. Follow through with a right punch of your own to the aggressor's head. Next, quickly release your left-hand hold on your opponent's arm, make a fist with your left hand, and snap it upward so that the back side of your knuckles hits the attacker. (This is called a *backfist strike.*)

Inward Block, Backfist, and Throw against an Angle Attack or Rear Attack

If you are attacked from an extreme side angle or from the rear, adjust your position so that you can clearly see your opponent. Even if your adversary attacks before you can directly face him or her, you can still defend yourself.

If you sense someone coming at you from far to the side or from the rear, step backward and bring your right forearm up to block and deflect his or her right-hand blow. Next, grab your opponent's punching arm with your left hand as you snap your right arm up at the elbow to hit your adversary on the side of the head with the back of your fist. Complete the action by pulling forward with your left hand on the captured arm as you step back with your left leg. This will draw your opponent's body across your right hip and enable you to slip your right hand around your opponent's body. Quickly twist your hips to the side as you continue to pull the attacker's captured arm down and over your hip, throwing him or her to the ground. You may finish with a kick.

Outward Block and One-Knuckle Punch against a Right Swing Punch

If an aggressor throws a right swing punch at you, you can deflect it by driving your left forearm out from near the center of your body. Follow up with a one-knuckle right-hand punch to the aggressor's solar plexus. Shift your weight onto your right leg as your left hand delivers a ridge-hand strike to the neck. Follow up, if necessary, by grabbing the aggressor's arms with your hands as you drive your right knee up and into the stomach or groin.

Escape, Kick, and Arm Bar against an Attempted Grab and Punch

An aggressor in an opposite stance (with the right side of his or her body forward) may grab your left wrist with his or her right hand and attempt to punch you with the left fist. If so, use your right hand to parry the incoming blow while you move to your left. Shift most of your weight onto your left leg so that, as you grab the aggressor's left wrist with your right (parrying) hand, you can raise your right knee and then kick the aggressor's knee.

After the kick, bring your right foot down behind your left leg so you are in a stable stance to the side of the aggressor's right arm. Free your left wrist by raising your left arm and slipping out of your opponent's grasp at the point where that person's thumb meets his or her finger. Quickly grab the aggressor's right wrist with your right hand and his or her arm with your left hand. Using both hands, turn that person's right arm so that his or her right elbow is facing up. Bend the aggressor's right wrist back as you slide forward and turn your body so that you are facing the same direction the attacker is facing.

While sliding and turning, maintain your hold on the aggressor's right hand with your right hand, and slide your left hand down to the elbow of the captured arm. Press down on the elbow with your left hand as you pull up and back on his or her wrist with your right hand.

1

2

3

5

4

6

Elbow Strike and Throw against a Rear Attack

An aggressor might grab you from the rear with his or her left hand in order to turn you around and deliver a right fist punch. If so, prevent the blow by stepping back toward the aggressor with your right leg and, as the attacker turns you around, delivering an outward block with your right forearm. Keep your left hand up for protection.

Once you have blocked the blow, bring your left hand down to grab the aggressor's right arm behind the elbow. At the same time, twist your body in to deliver a right elbow to the side of the opponent's neck, jaw, or head. Bring the captured right arm upward as you slip your head underneath it and move closer to the aggressor. Grab the person's legs with both hands and continue to drive forward as you pull his or her legs out to perform a takedown.

CLOSE-RANGE BLOWS

At close range, a taller person's longer limbs cease to be an advantage. For this reason, a smaller person might try to bring a fight into close range, hammer the larger opponent with a series of blows, and then pull away. During close-range fighting, circular punches, elbow strikes, hammer blows, palm-up punches, short kicks, knee attacks, and stamping kicks are very common. Grabbing actions, which are the start of a hold or take-down, are also launched from close range.

Skilled martial-arts practitioners learn not to fear dealing with an opponent at close range, but to take advantage of it to launch appropriate techniques. Beginning students of self-defense, however, should avoid starting out in this range.

Press Block and Palm-Heel Thrust against a Knee Attack

To keep an aggressor from hitting you in the groin with his or her left knee, press down with the palm of the hand closest to the attacking knee. Then, thrust the heel of your other hand outward with a turning motion, so that it hits the attacker under the chin. In practice sessions, *do not* actually make contact. Follow up by turning the hand that blocked the knee into a fist and using it for a palm-up punch to the aggressor's abdomen.

Parry and Arm Bar against a Hammer Blow

When an aggressor attempts to step forward with the right foot while delivering a hammer blow with the right fist, meet it from the inside with an outward, left-hand parrying action. Then grab your opponent's wrist with your left (parrying) hand. Slide forward and snap a right open-hand blow down on the bend of the elbow of the captured arm. Next, reach down with your right hand to grab the aggressor's right forearm. At the same time, step forward to bring your right foot behind your opponent's right leg. Then, using both hands, bend his or her right arm back. You may continue to apply this arm-lever action to keep the aggressor under control, or you may follow through with a takedown by kicking his or her right leg out.

Defense against a Circle Punch

If an aggressor is quite near and starts a right circle punch, thrust the heel of your left palm into his or her right bicep and follow through by extending your left arm almost straight out. Turn your right hip toward the aggressor and execute a right palm-up punch to the person's abdomen. With your left hand open, snap it out in a ridge-hand strike to drive the thumb edge into your opponent's neck. (A similar maneuver can be used against a left circle punch.)

Defense against a Right Ridge-Hand Strike

As an aggressor starts to throw a right ridge-hand strike, snap your left arm out with an open-hand blow so the bottom edge of your hand hits the bicep of the attacking arm. Follow up by striking down with the edge of your open left hand on the aggressor's neck.

Defense against a Palm-up Punch

When an aggressor launches a short, palm-up punch with the right arm, block it by thrusting your left arm downward to the crook of the attacking arm. Counterattack with your right arm by driving a one-knuckle-extended punch to the aggressor's solar plexus. Follow up, if necessary, with a left palm-up punch to his or her chin.

CLOSE-RANGE GRAPPLING

An aggressor at very close range could attempt to grab and wrestle you or to attack with a few blows. The blows may be less of a threat than is the grappling, because a blow from such close range may not gather enough momentum to do much harm. By learning to grapple, you can become an effective close-range fighter.

If you are stronger than your opponent or have skill in wrestling maneuvers, grappling will allow you to take advantage of your strong points. An opponent who prefers long-range punches and kicks might become disheartened if you force him or her to grapple.

Once you are in close to an opponent, keep your body stable and control your momentum to avoid being thrown off balance and becoming an easy target for a takedown. If possible, move behind an opponent so that he or she cannot easily attack.

An effective grappler gains force by using the full body—including arms, legs, and hips—to apply an escape or hold. While struggling with an aggressor, try to figure out his or her weak points and exploit them. Take advantage of any disruption in your opponent's balance by pulling or pushing that person in the direction he or she is already headed—countering a push with a pull and a pull with a push. In all grappling situations, stay calm, look for opportunities to escape from holds, and plan the moves you will use against your opponent once you break free.

Many of the techniques described in this section are *kansetsu-waza*—"locking techniques"—which can help you minimize the force needed to end a fight. Locking techniques should always be applied smoothly and quickly. Beginners should not try locking techniques in a real self-defense situation until they can be done with proper timing, speed, and form. Never apply a lock until you have first neutralized an aggressor's force. Sometimes you may need to distract such a person with a blow of your own before applying the lock. This will call for proper judgment on your part.

In practice sessions, never perform a lock on a partner who is not fully warmed up and aware of the technique to be applied. Make sure to practice locking techniques only under the supervision of a qualified instructor. Make your practice movements slow, continuous, and only forceful enough to let your partner begin to feel its effectiveness. Avoid rough or sudden actions during practice sessions, and arrange some kind of signal that your partner can use to indicate that it is time to ease up or release a lock.

The defenses in this section progress from elementary grappling maneuvers to more difficult ones. Do not underestimate the danger in basic attacks. If they are not handled correctly, you may end up in a precarious situation. Carefully practice all the defenses taught in this section and be ready to adapt them to any real-life confrontation.

Cross Arm Bar against a Side Grab

If you are side by side with an aggressor who tries to grab you with his or her left hand, capture the grabbing arm by the wrist with your left hand. Raise the captured arm and turn it palm-up. Reach under the uplifted arm with your right hand and grab the upper part of that person's body as you pull the attacking arm, palm-up, across your right arm. Bring the aggressor's left arm down so that the back of it near the elbow rests against your upper right arm. This action should place his or her left arm in a barred position that will be painful enough to stop further aggression.

Turn-over Arm Bar against a Grab

When an aggressor reaches out with his or her left hand, grab it with your left hand. While pulling your opponent's left arm straight, turn his or her left wrist over so the palm of the hand faces upward. Push your right hand down near the back of the elbow of the aggressor's overturned arm. If added pressure is necessary, press down with your right hand near or against the back of the elbow as you press back on the attacker's wrist with your left hand.

Hooking Arm Bar against a Frontal Grab

If an aggressor extends his or her left arm to grab you, turn your body to the outside of the reaching arm. Counterattack by grabbing the attacker's left wrist with your left hand. Turn the aggressor's left arm palm-up while you move your right leg forward and behind the aggressor's left leg. This should bring you around so that you and your opponent are both facing the same direction. At the same time, reach down and around the aggressor's left arm with a hooking motion of your right arm. Push down with your left hand on his or her wrist as you hold it palm-up and as you pull upward with your right arm.

Bent-Arm Bar against a Low Reaching Action

If an aggressor reaches out to grab you with his or her right hand, grab the wrist of the attacking right arm with your left hand. Pull your opponent's right arm out as you deliver an open-hand blow with the bottom edge of your right hand to the bend of his or her right elbow. Next, bring the aggressor's right arm up and back with your left hand while your right arm reaches down and around to grip the person's captured right arm. At the same time, take a deep step forward with your right foot as you use your opponent's bent right arm as a lever. Continue to pull the right wrist of the captured arm back and downward as you apply continuous pressure.

Defense against a Grab Action with Hammer Lock Counter from the Rear

If an aggressor moves forward to grab you with his or her hand, simply deflect the grabbing arm outward with your right hand and grab it. Follow up by grabbing your opponent's right wrist with your left hand. Get a firm grip under the attacking arm and twist the attacker's arm as you lift it up (rotating your grip as necessary for your comfort). Quickly slide your body under the captured arm and pivot so that you end up behind the aggressor and you are holding that person's right arm bent behind his or her back.

For extra leverage and security, bring your left hand up and around the aggressor's neck, getting a firm grip on the right shoulder as you pull the person tightly toward you. Gradually push the aggressor's right captured arm up his or her back as you tighten the hold with your other hand.

Escape and Straight-Arm Bar against a Chest Grab

If you are in a stance and an aggressor grabs your shirt at chest level with his or her left hand, grab the attacking left wrist with your left hand. As you do so, step with your right foot around his or her left leg, moving yourself slightly to his or her rear. During this motion, snap your right hand out with an open-hand blow over the aggressor's extended left arm to a sensitive area on his or her head or upper body. Next, grab the attacking left arm with both hands and turn it while you step fully behind your opponent so that you and he or she end up facing the same direction. Then quickly move your right hand to grasp the inner bend of your opponent's left elbow. As your right hand keeps that elbow from bending, use your left hand to pull your opponent's lower left arm into a straight-arm lock. Finish by sliding your right leg straight out in front of your opponent's left leg and kicking backward to throw the aggressor off balance.

Parry and Throw against a Choke Attempt

An aggressor's two-handed choke attempt should be deflected outward with a double parry (one that involves both of your palms). At the same time, step forward to place your right foot between your opponent's feet. Grab the aggressor's right arm with your left hand as you begin to slide your right arm around his or her neck. Then turn by pivoting on your right foot and press your back tightly against the front of your opponent. Bend your knees deeply, then snap up as you twist your body to the side and pull down on your opponent's captured right arm to throw him or her to the ground.

Reversal and Arm Lock from an Attempted Hammer Lock

If an aggressor approaches you from the rear and attempts a hammer lock by forcing your arm up your back, step forward and to the side with your leg to pull the opponent off balance. As you do so, deliver a backfist strike to his or her ribs or head. Step back with your foot as you swing the top half of your body down and around so you are facing the aggressor. Continue the direction of your movement as you twist your hips powerfully.

Keep your hands ready to block any attacks and use your arm's sweeping action to help break the attacker's grip. You should now be facing your opponent and standing to his or her right. Shift your weight to your right leg while you grab his or her right arm with both hands and bend it. Then place your left arm under his or her bent right arm near the elbow and trap it in a hammer lock by grabbing your left lower arm or wrist with your right hand. Apply pressure as necessary by tightening the hammer lock.

Wedge Block and Front Kick against a Double Grab

If an aggressor tries to grab your shirt with both hands, bring both of your hands up so that the soft part of your lower arm presses outward against his or her arms. Once you are freed from the aggressor's hold, snap a right front kick hard against that person's knee or shins. Follow up with a right punch to the middle level of your opponent's body and a left punch to the upper level.

Escape from a Rear Bear Hug

When an attacker reaches from behind to entrap you with both arms in a bear hug, take a deep breath to expand your chest. Then exhale while shooting your arms outward to loosen the grip. At the same time, spread your legs slightly. Next, place one of your legs (whichever is nearer to your opponent) behind the attacker. Then sweep that leg back toward you as the arm on the same side of your body pushes your opponent's upper body away from you.

Alternatively, just as you feel the bear hug being applied, you could kick backward with your right leg to try loosening the hold and then drive your arms upward to escape. If the hold is not broken by one of these tactics and the aggressor lifts you off the ground, move your legs as though you were running. Your opponent may not be able to hold on to you while you are moving so vigorously.

Escape from a Front Bear Hug

If an aggressor gets a double hand grip around you from the front and pulls you forward, continue moving as you push on your opponent. Quickly step forward with your leg and place it behind the aggressor's right leg as you press your body tightly against your opponent. Twist to the side while kicking the attacker's right leg out from underneath him or her to perform a throw.

An alternative is to drive your right knee into the aggressor's groin. Follow up, if necessary, by snapping out a series of short front kicks to the shins until the hold is released.

CHAPTER

9

FIGHTING ON THE GROUND

Fighting on the ground is a rather neglected area of self-defense training, even though the participants in many physical confrontations end up in this kind of combat. The Japanese masters, however, realized the importance of ground fighting and developed grappling techniques known as *katame-waza*.

Fast, protective action is a key principle of grappling. As soon as you are on the ground, take charge. Many of the techniques you can use are the same as those used when you are standing, but others are especially for fighting on the ground.

When attempting to escape from an attacker's hold, never bend your back in unnatural ways or try to use your neck as a lever to gain force for an escape. Also, do not depend too much on your arms when you are on the ground. Instead, use smooth, natural motions with your full body, including your legs, arms, and hips. The moment an adversary starts a lock or hold on your arm, it will probably make sense either to shoot your arm out or to recoil it, but you should also be ready to use the rest of your body to escape.

Unfortunately, an escape may not result from one or two simple moves. You may have to shift your body weight while throwing an aggressor off with a series of actions involving both your arms and your legs. No matter what series of moves you use, try to end up either on top with your opponent in a hold or safely standing away from him or her.

You should follow a few general principles in your ground fighting. Neutralize an aggressor's attack before you try to apply any hold or lock. Never try to apply an arm bar or wrist lock on a moving arm. When applying a hold, maintain complete control over your body. If you attempt to apply a joint lock on an aggressor and that person begins to escape by lifting your body, immediately release your lock so that you avoid counter pressure on your body. Giving up a hold or lock before it can be fully applied is no disaster; you can use plenty of other moves instead.

After you escape from an opponent's hold or lock, follow with a counterattack that will end the attacker's aggression. Take advantage of any vulnerable sensitive areas or any weaknesses in your opponent's position. Never use more force than is necessary. Brutality is not self-defense.

The techniques taught in this chapter are likely to be useful in common ground-fighting situations. Since grappling requires some sophistication, prepare not only by conditioning your body but also by taking a martial-arts class that will train you in ground-fighting techniques. Begin working on grappling skills only under the careful supervision of a qualified instructor.

Practice the various escapes, holds, and locks on both sides of the body. Also, in practicing holds or locks on a partner, only go through the motions of applying a technique. Never push hard against a partner's joint or limb. Use a safety system with your partner, a verbal or physical signal that a hold or lock should be released.

Countering a Side-Facing Aggressor's Punch

When an aggressor beside you on the ground threatens to punch, reach up with your left arm to block it. Then grab the wrist of the attacking arm with your left hand and grab the elbow of the attacking arm with your right. Pull the captured elbow back toward your body as you push the wrist of the attacking arm down, forward, and to the side so that you place him or her off balance with a variation of the bent-arm lock.

Defense against a Grab by a Front-Facing Aggressor

If an aggressor who is facing you on the ground reaches out to grab you with both hands, drive both of your arms up and outward. Reach across with your left hand and grab his or her left wrist. Place your right hand behind the aggressor's left elbow as you twist the left wrist with your left hand until the opponent's hand is turned palm-up. Press down on the left elbow with your right hand as you pull up on his or her left wrist. For added leverage, bend the aggressor's left wrist inward so that you have a combination arm lock and wrist lock.

Defense against a Hair Grab

If you are facing an aggressor on the ground and he or she reaches up with one hand to grab your hair, place both of your hands against the wrist of the reaching arm. Bend the hand backward at the wrist until you have the attacker in a wrist lock.

Defense against a Short Punch to the Abdomen

If an aggressor moves forward with a short left punch to your abdomen, parry the blow inward with your right hand. Next, grab the attacking left wrist with your right parrying hand and bring your body across the attacker's left arm as your left hand grips his or her arm to turn it palm-up. Now push back on the wrist of the aggressor's captured arm as you pull upward on the arm itself. Press down on the elbow of the captured arm, so you have your opponent in a straight-arm lock and wrist lock.

Defense against a Punch to the Head when Facing an Aggressor

If an aggressor throws a right punch at your face, bring your left arm up to meet it from the inside and block it outward. Grab the right wrist with your left hand while your right hand reaches up and grabs the elbow of that punching arm. Now pull the attacking wrist down and to the side as you direct the captured elbow inward and slightly up. End by applying a bent-arm lever lock.

Defending against a
Two-Hand Rear Choke

If you are seated on the ground and an aggressor begins to choke you from the rear, reach up to grab the small fingers of his or her hands and pull outward.

Alternatively, as the aggressor brings his or her hands around to choke you, reach up and across your body to grab that person's right wrist with your left hand. Twist the captured hand so that the aggressor's fingers are pointing up. Then continue to move your opponent's right hand away. Place your right hand on the palm of the captured hand and twist outward, placing him or her in an outward wrist lock.

Escape from a One-Arm Choke
from Behind

If an aggressor behind you on the ground places one hand around your neck, reach up quickly with the hand nearest the attacking arm and grip it near the attacker's shoulder. At the same time, grab his or her attacking wrist with your other hand. Shift forward the hip on the same side as the aggressor's captured limb while you move slightly upward, bend down at the waist, and pull down on the captured arm. This motion should, if smoothly and quickly performed, create enough momentum to throw the aggressor over your shoulder to the ground. If necessary, follow with a punch.

Escape and Arm Bar Counter against a Two-Hand Choke while on your Back

If your opponent is between your legs and choking you, drive a left palm-heel thrust to the side of his or her head. Next, reach across with your right hand and grab the aggressor's right wrist. As you do so, bend your right leg and raise it so that you can place the bottom of your foot against your opponent's left knee. Push against the knee while turning your body to the right, so that you force the aggressor face-down onto the ground. Bring your left foot over and place it on top of his or her right arm. Raise your body so that your weight rests on both your left foot and your right knee. Pull up on the aggressor's right arm and bend the wrist back. Then place your left hand on your opponent's elbow and push his or her right wrist back so that you have your opponent in a combination straight-arm bar and wrist lock.

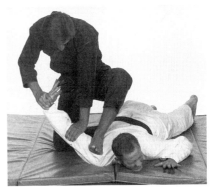

Straight-Arm Lock from the Ground

In some cases when you are forced to the ground by an aggressor, you will be able to sit up quickly while his or her back is still against the ground. If, in such a case, the aggressor reaches up to grab you, seize the reaching arm with both hands and shift so that you are sitting at his or her side. Grip the attacking arm at the wrist with one hand and put your other hand on the upper arm. Now place your right foot beside the aggressor's neck and roll backward as you lift your opponent's arm so that it is between your knees, with the elbow against your lower abdomen. Apply a straight-arm lock. Bring your knees together on his or her arm and apply pressure against the elbow until he or she submits.

Arm Coil-Lock from the Ground

If, in going to the ground, your opponent lands on his or her back, shift your weight so that you can fall across the upper half of his or her body. Grab your opponent's left wrist with your left hand, slide your right arm under his or her captured arm near the elbow, and grab your own left wrist with your right hand. Apply pressure by pulling back with your left hand while raising your right arm. Continue to press down on your opponent's body while using your right arm as a lever. Keep both of your knees on the ground, one next to the aggressor's shoulder and the other next to his or her abdomen.

and press the straightened arm against you. At this time, both of your hands should be putting pressure on the aggressor's straightened arm at the elbow. Continue the pressure by bringing this captured and straightened arm toward your chest with a steady movement back and to the side.

Straight-Arm Lock from a Sitting Position with Aggressor on Side

If your opponent is lying on his or her side, quickly move to sit next to him or her. Bend your left arm and slip it around whichever of your opponent's arms is not on the ground. Keep your left forearm across that captured arm just above the elbow, and straighten that arm as you grab your left hand with your right hand. Rest your left knee against the arm that your opponent has on the ground,

Takedown when on Knees against a Standing Aggressor

When you are on your knees and an aggressor is bearing down on you from a standing position, quickly drive your head into or alongside that person. At the same time, reach between the aggressor's legs and grab his or her right heel in your left hand as you grip the left ankle from the outside with your right hand. Quickly push your shoulders forward as you pull the aggressor's legs toward you to perform a takedown. Once he or she has been thrown to the ground, execute a blow to a sensitive area of the body.

Escape and Reversal when the Aggressor is on Top Facing the Same Direction

If you should end up on your knees with an aggressor on top of you facing the same direction, quickly move your body to the left. Grab your opponent's left ankle with your left hand, and pull on the left leg of the aggressor as you push forward with your left shoulder. This should drive your opponent onto his or her side. Rise sharply, using your body weight and hands to force the aggressor onto his or her back.

Escape and Arm Bar when on Knees with Aggressor in Front

When you are on your knees on the ground with an aggressor's arms bearing down, quickly grab that person's left wrist with your left hand. Bring your right arm up from under his or her left arm and pull it close to your body to trap the aggressor's left arm against you. Bring your right shoulder down as you twist your body to throw your opponent onto his or her back. Pull forward on the aggressor's captured left wrist with your left hand, so the attacker's arm is palm facing up, as your bent right arm puts pressure on his or her left elbow. You should end up with a straight-arm bar on the aggressor.

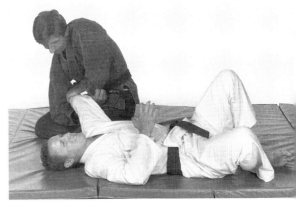

Escape when on Knees with Aggressor Alongside

When you are on your knees and an aggressor beside you is trying to turn you over, quickly clamp your left arm around his or her left arm. Trap this captured arm tightly against your body. Bring your left shoulder down as you turn and roll to draw your opponent over your body. Keep rolling until that person's back is forced to the ground. Finish by delivering a blow to a sensitive area.

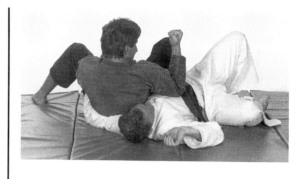

CHAPTER

10

STRATEGY

Your best self-defense strategy is to stay away from situations that call for fighting. Unfortunately, some battles cannot be avoided. When you have to fight, accept the situation and take immediate action to protect yourself. The Japanese masters, aware that nature's harmony may be disrupted by a storm, have advised people to adapt to adversity just as a willow bends to throw off even the heaviest snow.

GENERAL STRATEGIC PRINCIPLES

The following are principles that will help you adapt to a physical struggle with another person.

1. Maintain a correct mental posture.

Accept that sometimes you will be in conflict with other people. In such situations, control your attitude and avoid thinking about possible physical harm. Breathe evenly and naturally to control tension. Concentrate on what your opponent is doing, not on how you feel about it.

2. Adapt to the setting.

In order to mount an adequate defense, take stock of your surroundings. Understand where you can move and what obstacles may confront you. As you size up the setting, do not take off your coat, turn your back, or otherwise leave yourself open to an attack. Instead, keep your eyes on your potential opponent at all times.

Do not allow yourself to be backed into a corner unless you have superior grappling skills. Be wary of a sneak attack, such as a sucker punch when you are off guard. Once you know that a fight is unavoidable, assume a stance that seems appropriate against your opponent.

3. Consider distance.

Even your opponent's most powerful technique cannot harm you if it cannot reach you. Place yourself far enough away to avoid the full force of your opponent's blows yet close enough to counterattack. With well-chosen stances and movements, you can close or expand distance as you need to. Do not be caught off guard by an opponent who leads with one attack and quickly changes to another from an unexpected distance. Also, avoid moving so far back that you cannot counterattack. Simple evasion generally will not end a fight.

Adjust the distance between you and your opponent depending on what you want to achieve. If you are defending against long-

range techniques such as punches or kicks, stay no farther than just beyond the aggressor's longest blow or at an angle that makes it difficult for that person to reach you. You want to be able to move into long range or close range to throw your own punches, but you do not want to get so near that your opponent can easily grab you. If you decide to move into close range to take your opponent down or apply a hold or lock, first neutralize any attack by your opponent.

4. Choose your angle of attack.

The angle of your attack may make the difference between an effective technique and one that is simply evaded or blocked. To make your blows count, hit your opponent by surprise when and where he or she is vulnerable. For example, come in from the side or from the rear so that your opponent does not expect the attack and cannot turn quickly to defend.

At other times, you can set up an angled attack by deflecting an opponent's blow across his or her own body. This will direct your opponent's momentum away from you and will leave him or her temporarily unable to turn quickly to defend against any of your blows.

5. Exploit an opponent's vulnerabilities.

Each of your opponents will have particular strengths but also special weaknesses—for instance, in how the hands are held, in undefended openings, in balance while executing techniques, and even in breath control. An opponent may have a momentary lapse, or suki, after completing a technique, a push, or a pull, or when simply catching his or her breath. Against a skilled aggressor, however, you may have to create weaknesses by faking, forcing an overcommitment, or hitting from an angle.

PSYCHOLOGICAL DEFENSE TACTICS

By harnessing the full power of your mind and spirit—your greatest self-defense tools—you can vastly increase your ability to respond and to confuse even a strong or talented adversary. From the beginning of any confrontation, seize the psychological edge by remaining visibly confident and unafraid of the possibility of attack. Without bragging or trying to impress an adversary (which would only encourage that person to test your ability), try to keep him or her mentally off balance.

You can distract an aggressor with a simple hand motion, with an unexpected yell, by throwing an object, or by faking one type of attack as you launch another. For example, you might throw a high punch toward an opponent's face to attract attention while your other hand follows through with a punch to that person's solar plexus.

Techniques to distract and confuse an opponent can be useful when, in a prolonged confrontation, you cannot easily find openings in your opponent's defenses. To penetrate his or her guard, try pretending to be vulnerable to an attack. Once you have lured your opponent into making the expected moves, follow through with your defense and a counterattack. Another way of tricking your opponent into leaving an opening is to attack him or her in a way that will draw a predictable block and counterattack. Once you have handled his or her expected moves, strike out with a powerful blow of your own.

Making an Opening by Encouraging a Counterattack

If you know that a powerful aggressor usually blocks face punches upward and then counterattacks to the chest, encourage the counterattack by throwing a punch to his or her face. Deflect the expected counterattack out and away from your body to throw the aggressor off balance and then launch a punching attack of your own. This type of set-up maneuver—or some other form of distraction—is essential in dealing with aggressors who leave very few natural openings.

Making an Opening by Creating a Distraction

To create openings for attack, use techniques to distract the opponent from your real objective. For example, distract a powerful aggressor by throwing a quick jab, and then step toward the aggressor. Your jab should distract your opponent and allow you to get close enough to execute a throw. Bend down to grab your opponent's legs and pull them out from underneath him or her.

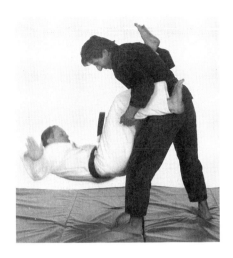

USE OF COMBINATIONS

The Japanese masters realized that many fights are not ended by one single technique. It may be necessary for one technique to be followed by another before an attacker's aggression ends. A fighter who relies on a simple block-and-punch combination to end a fight will be disappointed over and over again, as a strong aggressor absorbs the punch and fights back vigorously. A combination of techniques that can confuse the aggressor and can deliver a decisive technique is often needed to end a confrontation.

Certain styles of ju-jutsu teach a certain series of moves to use against a particular type of attack. For example, a defender might first distract an aggressor with a hand strike to the head and then follow with a hold and a throw. In using such combinations, adjust your aim so that they do not always strike the same general area of the opponent's body. Practice punching and striking at high, middle, and low targets on an opponent's body. Also practice executing hand and foot techniques from different angles.

In a real fighting situation, you might, once you are inside an aggressor's guard, be able to end a fight by throwing a quick series of blows. You might also be able to end a fight by neutralizing an aggressor's attacking limb, executing a blow, and following up with a hold, lock, or a throw.

STRATEGIC OPTIONS IN HANDLING AN AGGRESSOR

Traditional martial-arts strategy developed from the conditions of actual warfare. The early samurai, whether they were fighting hand-to-hand or with weapons, had to determine not only what type of aggressor they faced but also how to time their attack. The three basic choices that they recognized are still valid in modern real-life confrontations—as long as you remember that modern society allows only reasonable force in repelling an attack. Using unnecessary or excessive force, even in self-defense, can get you in a lot of trouble, so be careful and exercise self-control.

Instant Attack

An instant attack is launched while someone who started the fight is preparing for further aggression. By moving quickly and unexpectedly, you catch him or her off guard. An instant attack, however, should not start a fight but should only be a response to a physical confrontation that has already begun. You should never use force unless an aggressor's actions clearly indicate that he or she means to harm you—and even then you must use only a reasonable amount of force.

The principle of the instant attack can have a wider application against everyday difficulties. Take immediate action to take care of a problem—including any of your emotional difficulties or bad habits—before it causes serious harm.

Waiting Attack

In this type of defense, a defender lets an attack dissipate before countering. The defender waits for the suki, or gap, at the end of the attack, when the aggressor is off balance or otherwise vulnerable. This type of defense is only effective if you can quickly exploit any gaps with an effective counterattack. This requires attention to rhythm and timing, so that the aggressor is allowed to drain away energy on the failed attack, energy that is then redirected against him or her. This type of defense is probably most often used in certain styles of ju-jutsu.

Like most strategies, this one has to be used wisely. If it becomes predictable, it will fail to draw your opponent into the position you want to exploit. Also, like many other lessons of the Japanese masters, this principle has broader applications. In business or in debate, it is often wise to wait for a competitor to make a broad statement that can later be taken apart, bit by bit, to show its weakness.

Body-to-Body Attack

This type of self-defense strategy is used in close-range fighting when the aggressor is out of balance or is caught off guard. Once again, timing is key. Once an attack has started, quickly take advantage of any temporary gap in the aggressor's defenses by launching your own fighting maneuvers, especially from an unexpected angle or in a unique way. For example, if an aggressor starts to move forward with grabbing action, you can move in close and hit unexpectedly with a blow to a sensitive area. Your sudden move should put a halt to the aggressor's action. Like other strategies, this one should be used with no more force than is necessary and only when you are sure that an opponent means to do you harm.

HANDLING DIFFERENT TYPES OF AGGRESSORS

Although you must adapt a defense for each physical confrontation, certain guidelines and tactics can help you handle some common types of opponents. Aggressors of any personality type generally have certain tactics, strengths, and weaknesses in common.

This section outlines six basic types of aggressors and suggests ways of dealing with them. As you follow these suggestions, however, keep in mind the basic defense principles, your strengths in self-defense, and any individual characteristics you observe in your opponent.

The Street Fighter

Proud of being rough and unpredictable, the street fighter should be carefully watched as long as he or she is near. This type of fighter is likely to try catching you off guard with a sucker punch or hitting you when your back is turned. Never take off your coat while talking to such a person or move in a way that would leave you off balance. Recognize that a street fighter generally relies on wild, swinging punches in combination with low kicks. Evade such attacks by moving to the side, so that the attacker's energy is wasted. Try to confuse the street fighter by slipping behind him or her—a safe position for you and a vulnerable one for your opponent.

If you are face-to-face against such an individual, do not lead off with a circular hand attack unless you are so close that a straight punch may not gather momentum. Even though circular blows can pack a lot of power and can catch an opponent off guard, a straight blow will usually hit a target more quickly than a circular one. If the street fighter throws a wild swing or circular punch at the same time you throw a straight punch, yours will probably hit first.

If your opponent is an experienced fighter, he or she may try to catch you off guard by charging forward with a series of explosive blows to vulnerable areas. Either evade this charging attack at an angle and follow with a counterattack, or unexpectedly explode forward with your own well-placed blows to open areas on the attacker. When moving in on the attacker, use fast, straight lead techniques that enable you to close distance while keeping your attacking limb between you and him or her. Your lead technique should create

an opening for your follow-up techniques.

If your response does not end the fight, move away and assume a stable stance and a determined look. Be ready for the street fighter's next attack. If the aggressor does move in again, use a different defense and counterattack to avoid being predictable. Keep a stable stance throughout the confrontation. Move far enough away so that the aggressor's attack misses you, but stay close enough to execute quick counterattacks. Use blocks that both deflect the blow and throw your opponent off balance.

A street fighter usually has only one or two successful techniques that he or she repeats in each fight. Once you know what these techniques are, you can easily counter them with an appropriate defense. If, at the start of a fight, you do not know what an aggressor's favorite techniques are, look for them during the fight. If you can withstand the street fighter's favorite techniques, he or she might just give up the fight. If your opponent persists, concentrate your energy on powerful combinations to sensitive areas of the body until the fight ends.

The Loud Aggressor

Some people enjoy bragging. Their noise and annoying antics, however, show a lack of self-confidence and a great need for attention. Generally, you should simply ignore one of these loud persons and walk away, but if you cannot do so without being attacked, size up his or her weaknesses. For example, a lot of hand-waving and threatening gestures will leave an opponent in a fairly weak body position and with an unsteadiness you can exploit.

Once the actual physical confrontation has begun, deflect any attacking limbs away from you and across the aggressor's body, so that he or she is swept off balance. Immediately follow by hitting a sensitive area. A loud aggressor is likely to be so surprised by your strong defensive action that he or she will quit fighting.

The Grappler

Some people enjoy grabbing or wrestling with other people. If you are forced into a confrontation with a grappler, do not despair. The overconfidence common among grabby aggressors often leaves them open to counterattack. The grappler expects most people to either give up easily or try to match wrestling skill. Do not try to match the grappler's strength or grappling technique. Instead, hit such an aggressor at available openings.

If you cannot move away, dodge and follow through with a series of blows to sensitive areas. Never move directly forward into a grappler's reach, but hit at the flanks, using angle attacks. Try to execute a decisive technique or move behind the opponent and counterattack from a relatively safe position.

A powerful punch or strike may not be enough to drop the grappler. Some powerful grapplers are willing to take a blow in order to get the opportunity to grab you and wrestle you to the ground. To avoid this trap, always withdraw quickly after hitting a grappler. Movement is the key against such an opponent, who probably expects people to just stand still and lock horns.

To avoid being off balance against a wrestler, throw kicks only to the knees or lower and quickly withdraw. If you are forced to fight in close, use a series of short palm-up blows, elbow strikes, knee kicks, and foot stamps. Also, exploit any opportunity to bend back one of your opponent's fingers or to apply a wrist lock. Sometimes simply pinching, bending back a finger, or striking a sensitive area will cause a grappler to release a hold. Your strategy should stress mobility and solid ground-fighting principles.

The Muscular Bully

A bully who is proud of his or her body might not have great athletic ability. A bully's big muscles do not necessarily indicate coordination, precise timing, or skill in self-defense. To handle such an aggressor, take a strong yet flexible stance.

The muscular bully relies upon his or her ability to deliver a blow that will end all resistance—perhaps a circular punch. If you throw a quick straight punch—especially from an angle—just as your opponent launches a circle punch, your blow will hit first and you will have the advantage.

Circle the muscular bully, and each time that person begins to launch a power punch, hit first with a straight punch of your own. If possible, follow with a combination of blows. In a prolonged confrontation, move around your opponent, varying the tempo and pattern of your blows. Try to catch the muscular bully off guard. Move in to attack and dart out quickly before your opponent can counterattack.

Never take a deep stance and slug it out or grapple with the muscular bully. Distance and timing are very important in mounting a successful defense. When the bully throws a punch or tries to grab you, evade and hit back in the gap before the next attack. Try to move so that the aggressor overextends his or her attacking limb and falls off balance. Execute a decisive technique when your opponent least expects it. Generally, the muscular bully lacks the psychological and physical endurance for prolonged fighting and tires quickly.

The Knock-out Specialist

The streets are full of make-believe Rocky Balboas—people who think they could have been world boxing champions. Usually you can simply ignore their antics, but sometimes you may be forced into a fight with one of these sluggers.

Knock-out specialists who bother or bully people are not ordinarily great fighters. (If they were, they would be in the ring, not starting fights at school or on the street.) Recognizing this weakness, you can concentrate on observing a knock-out specialist's moves so that you do not get caught off guard by a sucker punch or a series of sloppy blows.

As in any conflict, try to avoid a fight. If this is not possible, then assume a well-guarded stance that provides both stability and mobility. Once the fight begins, evade, parry, or block the aggressor's attacks.

Follow up defensive moves with a quick series of counterattacks and then withdraw.

Carefully observe the aggressor's movements and try to gauge the strength and timing of his or her blows. At the first opportunity, execute a series of quick kicks to the knees or shins, followed by a series of punches from an angle at which you are out of the knock-out specialist's reach.

You may win with a decisive blow or, if you are confident in your grappling skills, you might want to use a hold, lock, or throw after you deflect any attacks and put your opponent off balance. The knock-out specialist is likely to be uncomfortable wrestling on the ground and might, on recognizing that you are determined to grapple, lose his or her eagerness to fight.

The Kicking Specialist

The specialist in fancy kicks is a recent addition among Western fighters. Traditionally, kicks were frowned on in many parts of the world, but recent martial-arts movies have given bullies and would-be martial artists the idea that they can use high kicks and other fancy foot maneuvers. These techniques, however, are very difficult and leave the kicker off balance, so very few street fighters can use them successfully.

Try to force a kicking bully to fight at close range, where flashy long-range kicks or punches are useless. Even if an opponent does throw a kick at you, just evade it and then move in to punch or throw your opponent. You can also evade the opponent's kick and follow through with your own kick to his or her supporting leg. Once a fancy kicker has had his or her supporting leg hit a few times, he or she tends to shy away from kicking.

You can also keep the kicking specialist's feet on the ground by kicking him or her in the groin immediately after you evade an attack. When a kicking specialist retreats from your close-range counterattack, you can move after him or her with explosive hand and foot combinations. You may apply a hold, lock, or a throw after you deflect his or her attack. The kicking specialist may be defeated by a decisive technique or give up because of your willingness to fight at a close distance.

The Well-Rounded Adversary

Luckily, you will rarely encounter a well-rounded adversary. Skilled fighters tend to find no enjoyment in street fighting, since they have plenty of opportunity to prove their skill against other talented individuals in a more challenging and rewarding environment. If you believe, however, that your op-

ponent is the exception—a truly well-rounded adversary—then take a strong stance, clear your mind, and breathe naturally. Do not allow an adversary to frighten or enrage you. Once the confrontation has begun, keep your mind on the action, not on your opponent's supposed skills.

Even in dealing with a well-rounded adversary, you can mount excellent defenses and find openings to attack. Your adversary may be overconfident, and you may be able to gain an advantage by remaining calm and carefully observing his or her movements. To keep him or her from learning too much about you, avoid repeating your techniques. The moment you spot a weakness, try to execute a decisive technique quickly. If your opponent is clearly off balance, execute a throw that gains force from his or her own momentum. If you have immobilized one of your opponent's arms or legs, quickly apply a hold or lock that will end the fight.

As a basic strategy, do the things that you do well, and exploit any weaknesses of your opponent. Attack from an unexpected angle if your adversary is skilled at blocking. Keep changing your pattern, tempo, and rhythm of movement so it is difficult for your opponent to predict your next move. Try to direct your techniques at his or her blind or forward side, while you remain hard to reach with any blows from his or her strong rear side.

If your opponent evades your blows, vary the type and tempo of your movement as you move into a range where he or she can be hit. Use a confusing mix of movements to get close and around behind the opponent. From this position, execute a takedown.

If your adversary charges you with blows,

try to move away so you end up at a 45-degree angle to him or her. With fakes and other techniques, disrupt your opponent's combination attacks and try to confuse him or her. If your opponent is good at punching, evade to the side and kick at his or her knees or shins. By keeping your adversary unsure of what you are going to do, you can gain time to plan an effective strategy.

Never try to match a skilled fighter's speed. Instead, circle such a person—staying at his or her side and hitting from long range with jabs or kicks—so he or she cannot easily get at you. If possible, slip behind a dangerous adversary. Strike at sensitive areas or execute a throw once you are safely behind your opponent. Look for the opponent's suki, and strike with great force once it is available. Above all, be confident, calm, and persistent.

11

SUGGESTIONS
FOR TRAINING

The principles, techniques, and strategies outlined in this book are only the beginning of an effective self-defense program. It takes many years of hard work, practice, and determination to become skillful. The first step, as suggested earlier in this book, is to make sure that your body can meet the rigors of training.

Once you have a doctor's approval to begin training, seek out a qualified instructor who can introduce you to the fundamentals.

No book can ever take the place of proper personal instruction. Reinforce this instruction by first reading this book from beginning to end and then going back to study each lesson more carefully.

After a few weeks of conditioning, gradually begin to practice the basic techniques in this book. At first, put great emphasis on form. Each technique in a series should first be practiced slowly and individually. After you can perform it well, use it in combination with the others. To avoid physical strain, start slow and simple. Later, you can speed up, put together your own combinations of moves, and perform them at different ranges.

Before performing combinations on an actual person, be cleared for such training by your instructor. Do not practice falling techniques, throws, holds, or locks until you have learned them in a class under supervision. They have been included in this book simply to give you an outline of how they are done.

Never use the fighting techniques in this book against another person unless you need to in a real-life confrontation. Even then, use only enough reasonable force to end a confrontation. Carefully adhere to the suggestions that follow:

1. Before practicing any fighting techniques, do a full set of warm-up exercises.

2. Start out using techniques very slowly, concentrating on your form. Use a mirror to observe your form periodically. Using the photographs in this book as models, alter your form as necessary. Once your form is adequate, you can work on increasing your speed.

3. Stay loose and limber while practicing. Do not freeze up or start worrying about how you look to others in the practice room. When you are tense, you slow down and tire out more quickly.

4. Once you understand the basic aspects of a technique and can perform it accurately, combine it with others.

5. When working with a partner, always use safety equipment such as a headguard, mouthpiece, groin cup, and knee guards. Beginning students should practice techniques with a partner only under the careful supervision of a qualified instructor. Practice any grappling only on a thick mat designed for that purpose.

6. Do not let any of your punches or kicks actually hit your partner. Stop all blows at least 1 inch from his or her body. Contact is only for very advanced students wearing full safety gear and practicing under the direct supervision of a qualified instructor. Never even pretend to throw blows toward your practice partner's sensitive areas, such as the eyes, nose, throat, neck, ribs, groin, knees, or the area near the centerline of the back.

7. In practicing with a partner, do not put all of your force into a punch. Practice full-power techniques only on a punching bag.

8. Avoid the flashy techniques you see in movies. Concentrate on developing your skill in the basic techniques.

9. Squeeze your fist tightly just before hitting something. This will protect your hand and wrist.

10. Do not allow anyone to throw you in practice until you have developed excellent falling skills. Also, never throw anyone else unless he or she is trained to fall properly.

11. Never try to catch your partner off guard with a throw, sweep, hold, or lock in practice. Make sure your partner is ready before you execute any technique.

12. Thoroughly warm your body up before practicing any falling techniques.

13. Before either you or your partner applies any holds or locks, both of you must be warmed up, well stretched, and loose. Never apply a hold or lock on a joint that is sore, has a history of injury, or is chronically weak. Stop immediately at the first sign of any pain in a joint.

14. Work out a warning system with your partner to signal one another if a hold or lock is painful. On receiving that signal, release your partner immediately.

15. Do not rush your training, but move through it with patience and emphasis on quality of action. Try to enjoy each training session, as you gain skill one day at a time.

Index

About the Author

Fred Neff started his training in the Asian fighting arts at the age of eight. In 1974, Mr. Neff received a rank of fifth degree black belt in karate. The same year he was made a master of the art of kempo at a formal ceremony. He is also proficient in judo, jujutsu, and more than one style of chuan-fa. Mr. Neff's study of East Asian culture has taken him to Hong Kong, Japan, the People's Republic of China, and Singapore.

For many years, Mr. Neff has used his knowledge to educate others. He has taught karate at the University of Minnesota, the University of Wisconsin, Hamline University, and Inver Hills Community College in St. Paul, Minnesota. He has also organized and supervised self-defense classes for special education programs, public schools, private institutions, and city recreation departments. Included in his teaching program have been classes for law enforcement officers.

He has received many awards for his accomplishments and community involvement, including the City of St. Paul Citizen of the Month Award in 1975, a Commendation for Distinguished Service from the Sibley County Attorney's Office in 1980, the WCCO Radio Good Neighbor Award in 1985, the Lamp of Knowledge Award from the Twin Cities Lawyers Guild in 1986, and the Presidential Medal of Merit in 1990.

Fred Neff graduated with high distinction from the University of Minnesota College of Education in 1970. In 1976, he received his J.D. degree from William Mitchell College of Law in St. Paul, Minnesota. Mr. Neff is a practicing attorney in Minneapolis, Minnesota.

He is the author of 19 books, including

Everybody's Book of Self-Defense, Lessons from the Western Warriors, Lessons from the Eastern Warriors, Lessons from the Fighting Commandos, and the eight books that make up Fred Neff's Self-Defense Library.